ACE Mathematics 2

*13 exciting blackline activities
to engage ages 6-7*

David Smith

TarquinGroup
www.tarquingroup.com

Acknowledgements

Thanks are due to many people but especially to my lovely wife and also my dear mum who between them patiently played all the games with me to test their initial suitability. I also have to thank the teachers and children of Peel Park Primary School for giving them a road test, spotting my errors and making suggestions on how they could be further developed and improved. Finally thanks go to the staff at Tarquin, for their support in the editing process.

Dedication

This book is dedicated to the memory of Maxine Firth, an inspirational friend and colleague who shared my ideal of an enjoyment of mathematics for all.

Published by Tarquin Publications
Suite 74, 17 Holywell Hill
St Albans
AL1 1DT

www.tarquingroup.com

Copyright © David Smith, 2014
ISBN: 978-1-907-55092-8

Distributed in the USA by IPG Books
www.ipgbooks.com
www.amazon.com & major retailers

Distributed in Australia by OLM www.lat-olm.com.au

All rights reserved. Sheets may be copied singly for use by the purchaser only, or for class use under a valid school or institutional licence from the relevant Copyright Licensing society.

Introduction

'By the end of year 2, pupils should know the number bonds to 20...and the 2, 5 and 10 multiplication tables....An emphasis on practice at this early stage will aid fluency.'
Key Stage 1 National Curriculum Programme of Study

'The teacher created a positive climate for learning in which pupils were interested and engaged.'

OFSTED Inspector

Welcome to a world of mathematical fun and games!

Easy to play and requiring only basic equipment, these educational games engage even the most reluctant of learners whilst boosting confidence for all.

Great for teachers, intervention workers, teaching assistants, private tutors and parents, the flexible nature of this game pack offers:

▶ practice for specific objectives from the new National Curriculum

▶ a great resource to:
   "ensure students are engaged in learning and generate high levels of commitment to learning"
      (Outstanding Grade Descriptors, *Ofsted School Inspection Handbook* (updated 2014))

▶ the opportunity to demonstrate a commitment to:
   "the social development of pupils at the school" within curriculum time
            (Ofsted Framework for School Inspection (updated 2014))

▶ an effective assessment tool

▶ the promotion of problem solving and thinking skills through game strategy

▶ fun homework activities

Playing Information

All these games require a pack of playing cards and most also need some kind of coloured counters or other objects such as beads or buttons. Suitable materials are available from Tarquin - see page 40 for details. When the picture cards are used the jack represents number eleven, the queen is number twelve and the king is thirteen. To help children remember this you may want to consider writing the actual numbers in the corners of each card.

And that's all you need to know to enjoy years of happy gaming!

David Smith

Hexums

Focus

Hexums is a game for two or three players which practices recall of facts for the 2, 5 and 10 multiplication tables.

What you need

▶ Playing cards (kings removed)

▶ Counters (a different colour for each player)

▶ Hexums game board

How to play

When the kings have been removed from the pack the remaining cards are shuffled and placed in a pile, face-down and within reach of all the players. Player 1 turns over a playing card from the pack and places it face-up in front of them. The number on the card is then multiplied: by two if playing Hexums 2, by five in Hexums 5, and by ten in Hexums 10.

For example (Hexums 2)

Player 1 turns over a six so must say 6 x 2 = 12. After saying the correct answer Player 1 can place a counter on any of the matching answers on the game board.

Player 2 then turns over a card and multiplies the number by two. This time a queen is turned over so Player 2 says 12 x 2 = 24 and can also place a counter on any of the matching answers on the game board.

Players continue to take cards in turn, multiply the number on the card and place their counters on the board. If a player gives an incorrect answer they are not able to place a counter on that turn.

How to win

Each player has to try and make a continuous line of coloured counters on adjacent numbers from the outer ring to the inner ring of shaded hexagons, as shown in the diagram.

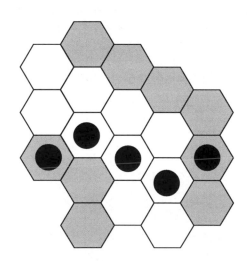

Rule changes / Next steps

▶ Limit the players to twelve counters each to try and get a winner.

▶ Record multiplication facts on paper or a whiteboard. At the end of the game use these to generate other multiplication and division facts (as below) and then test each other.

| 6 x 2 = 12 | so | 12 = 2 x 6 | 12 ÷ 2 = 6 | 2 = 12 ÷ 6 |
| 12 x 2 = 24 | so | 24 = 2 x 12 | 24 ÷ 2 = 12 | 2 = 24 ÷ 12 |

Instruction Sheet © Tarquin Photocopiable under licence – for terms see page 2

Hexums
x 2

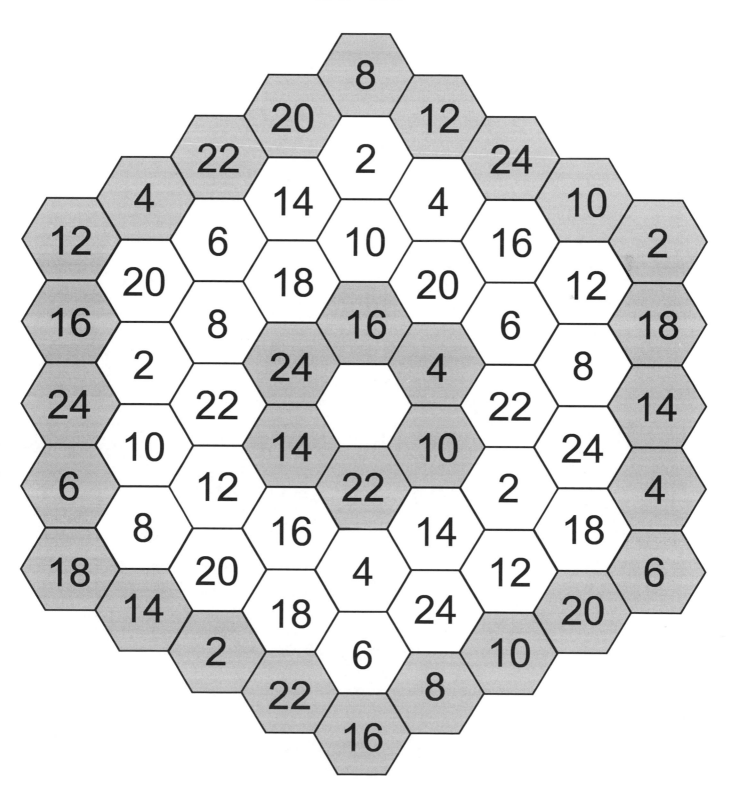

Game Board © Tarquin Photocopiable under licence – for terms see page 2

Hexums

x 5

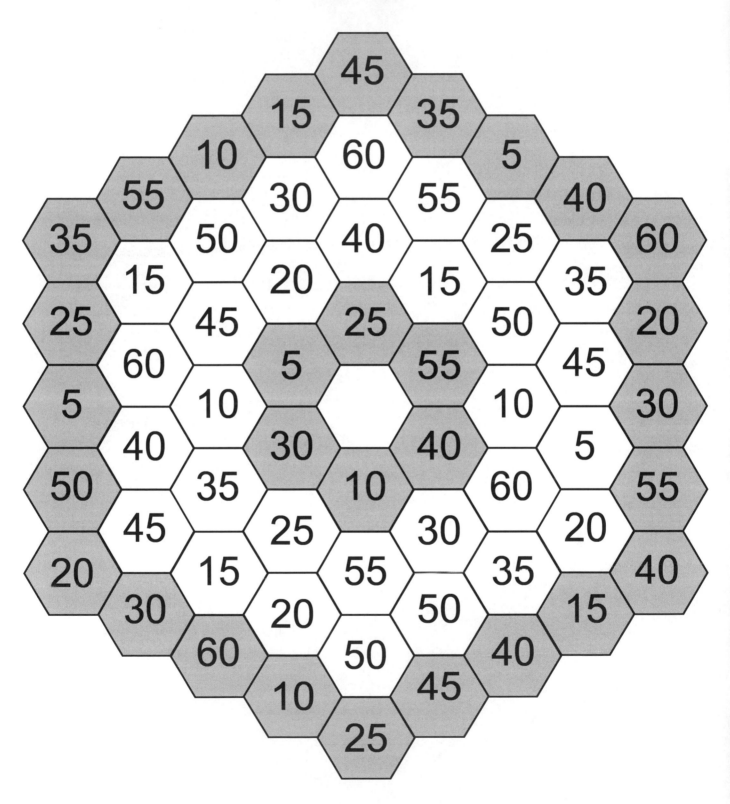

Hexums
x 10

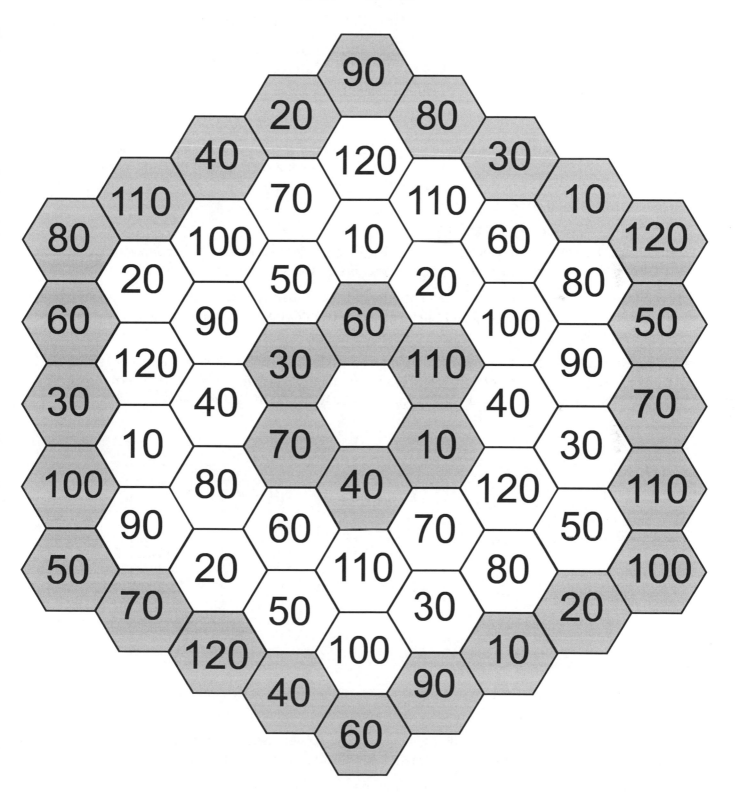

Square Up

Focus

Square Up is a game for two to four players which practices recall of multiplication facts for the 2, 5 and 10 multiplication tables.

What you need

▶ Playing cards (kings removed)

▶ Counters (a different colour for each player)

▶ Square Up game board

How to play

When the kings have been removed from the pack the remaining cards are shuffled and placed in a pile, face-down and within reach of all the players. Player 1 turns over a playing card from the pack and places it face-up in front of them. The card is then multiplied: by two if playing Square Up 2, by five in Square Up 5, and by ten in Square Up 10.

For example (Square Up 2)

Player 1 turns over an eight so must say 8 x 2 = 16. After saying the correct answer Player 1 can place a counter on any of the matching answers on the game board.

Player 2 then turns over a card and multiplies the number by two. This time a jack is turned over so Player 2 says 11 x 2 = 22 and can also place a counter on any of the matching answers on the game board.

Players continue to take cards in turn, multiply the number on the card and place their counters on the board. If a player gives an incorrect answer they are not able to place a counter on that turn. A player may turn over another card if no matching answer can be found on the game board.

How to win

Players have to make the shape of a square, by placing counters on each corner, as shown in the diagram.

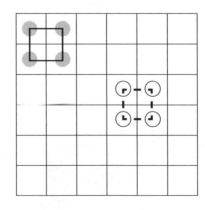

Rule changes / Next steps

▶ Players score four points for each square they make and play can continue until all their counters have been used or until there are no spaces left on the game board.

▶ Make some flashcards showing the multiplication or division facts on one side and the answer on the other side. Children can then use them for individual practice or to test a partner.

▶ Allow players to make larger squares to win the game as long as they have a counter on each corner.

Instruction Sheet © Tarquin Photocopiable under licence – for terms see page 2

SQUARE UP 2

12	20	8	2	16	10
22	16	4	6	14	20
18	24	10	12	2	4
2	14	20	8	18	22
10	16	22	16	24	14
24	8	18	4	6	18

Game Board © Tarquin Photocopiable under licence – for terms see page 2

SQUARE UP 5

35	55	20	50	15	5
5	25	10	45	55	60
60	20	40	30	35	25
15	10	50	5	40	45
40	30	35	15	60	20
45	25	55	10	25	50

SQUARE UP 10

70	60	110	80	50	120
90	120	30	20	60	10
20	40	10	50	100	70
100	80	90	110	40	30
120	30	60	70	20	110
40	50	100	10	80	90

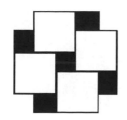

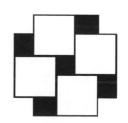

Target

Focus

Target is a game for two or more players which practices recall of addition and subtraction facts up to thirteen.

What you need

▶ Playing cards

▶ Target game board

▶ How to play

Before play can begin, a target number must be chosen by turning over a card from the top of the pack. In this example, the target number chosen is nine. Three cards are then turned over and placed face-up in each space on the game board. The rest of the cards are dealt out equally between the players and are then placed face-down in a pile in front of them, as shown in the diagram below.

Player 2

TARGET

Player 1

Player 3

Player 1 then turns over a card from their pile and looks to see if they can use this number with one of the numbers on the game board to make nine. Player 1 first turns over a seven and places it on top of the two of clubs as 7 + 2 = 9. Then Player 1 turns over an ace and places it on top of the eight of spades as 8 + 1 = 9. Player 1 then turns over a six, as shown in the diagram, and a total of nine can't be made. When this happens the card is placed face-up next to their pile and it is the end of their turn.

Player 2

TARGET

Player 1

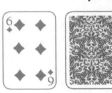

Player 3

Instruction Sheet © Tarquin Photocopiable under licence – for terms see page 2

Player 2 then turns over a card and tries to find a combination of numbers to make the target number. In this example Player 2 turns over a three of spades. This card can be placed on top of the queen of clubs as 12 − 3 = 9. Player 2 then turns over the ten of clubs and can place it on top of the ace of hearts as 10 − 1 = 9. Next a four is turned over but this can't be used to make the target number, so Player 2's turn ends.

Player 3 then takes their turn. The first card turned over is the five of hearts which can't be placed on the target game board to make nine. However, the card can be placed on top of Player 2's four of diamonds as 4 + 5 = 9. Player 3 can then turn over another card to see if it can be placed on the game board or on top of another player's pile. This time it is a king so Player 3's turn comes to an end.

When players have their next turn they can look at their face up card first to see if that can be put anywhere before turning a card over. Player 1 can therefore put their six on top of the three as 3 + 6 = 9.

How to win

The first player to use all the cards in their pile is the winner. If the players get to a point where they all still have cards in their pile but none of them can take a turn, the player with the fewest number of cards is the winner.

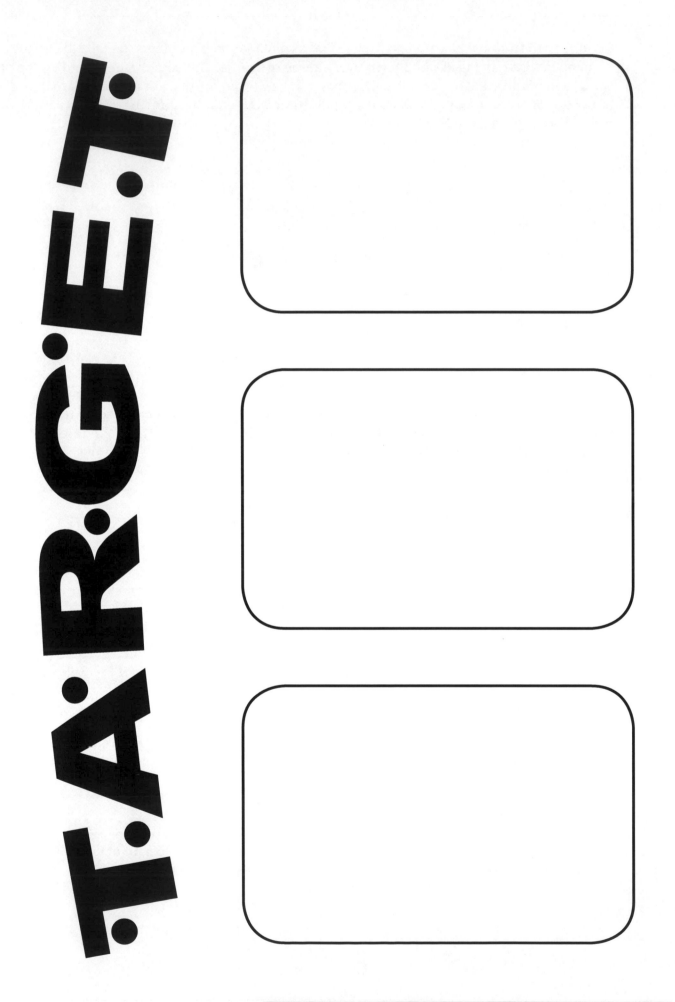

Get Rid!

Focus

Get Rid is a game for two or more players which practices recall and use of addition and subtraction facts with numbers up to fifteen.

What you need

▶ Playing cards

▶ Whiteboard / paper and pen

How to play

Before play can begin, a Get Rid number must be chosen by the players. Player 1 can be asked to pick a random number between zero and fifteen or a card can be turned from the top of the pack. In this example the number chosen is seven. After shuffling the cards Player 1 deals out three to each player and places the rest of the pack face-down and within reach of all the players.

Players must then look at their cards and try to find out how they can add or subtract to make a total of seven. As Player 1 dealt the cards Player 2 goes first and must pick up a card from the top of the central pile to start their turn. They then see if they can use any of their cards to make the Get Rid number.

For example

$5 + 2 = 7$

$8 - 1 = 7$

$2 + 2 + 3 = 7$

If they can find a set, the cards are placed down for other players to see and check that they are correct. If they can't find a set of cards to make the Get Rid numbers they must wait to pick up another card on their next turn. Play continues with players picking up cards in turn and trying to make the Get Rid number. Players score 10 points for each set of cards making the Get Rid number.

Play continues until one of the players 'Gets Rid' of all of their cards. If no player is able to use all their cards in this way then the round ends when all the cards in the pile have been used. The player who puts down all their cards receives a Get Rid bonus of 10 points. All the other players have to take away two points for each card they still have left in their hand.

Record the scores for the round using a whiteboard or paper and pen and then play again. Set a different Get Rid number for the next round.

How to win

The winner is the player with the most points after an agreed number of rounds.

Rule changes / Next steps

▶ Allow players to use an ace with another card to make a two-digit number, such as an ace and a five to make fifteen.

▶ Allow players to do simple multiplication and division as well as addition and subtraction to help make the Get Rid number, such as $10 \div 5 + 5 = 7$.

Instruction Sheet © Tarquin Photocopiable under licence – for terms see page 2

Worms

Focus

Worms is a game for two or more players which practices recall of addition and subtraction facts up to twenty.

What you need

▶ Playing cards (picture cards removed)

▶ Counters (different colour for each player)

▶ Worms game board

How to play

When the picture cards have been removed the remaining cards are placed face-down in a pile within reach of all the players. Player 1 turns over two cards and must either add the value of the cards together to find the total or subtract the smaller value from the larger to find the difference.

For example

Player 1 turns over a six and a nine, they can say $6 + 9 = 15$ or $9 - 6 = 3$. They can then place a counter on either of the matching answers on the game board.

Player 2 then turns over two cards and has to say the total or the difference. Turning over a queen and a seven, they have to say either nineteen or five, as $12 + 7 = 19$, and $12 - 7 = 5$. On giving one of these correct answers they can place a counter on that number on the game board.

Players continue to take turns saying the total of or the difference between their two cards, and covering the matching answers on the game board. Each player must try and make a worm by placing counters on adjacent squares, as shown in the diagram. If a player can't make an answer on the game board they miss that turn.

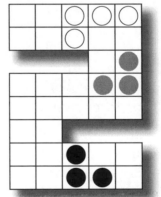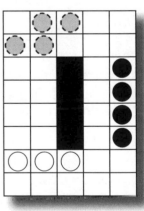

How to win

For two or three players, the first to get a four-worm on adjacent squares wins the game, but for more than three players, a three-worm can win.

Rule changes / Next steps

▶ Players may find it useful to have a whiteboard/paper and pen so they can write each possible calculation down and work out both answers before deciding where to place their counter.

▶ You could also allow play to continue until all the squares on the board have been covered, or a set number of counters used, especially if there are only two players. Then add up the final score for each player to decide the winner using the following points:

3 square worm = 2 points
4 square worm = 5 points

5 square worm = 10 points
6 square worm = 20 points

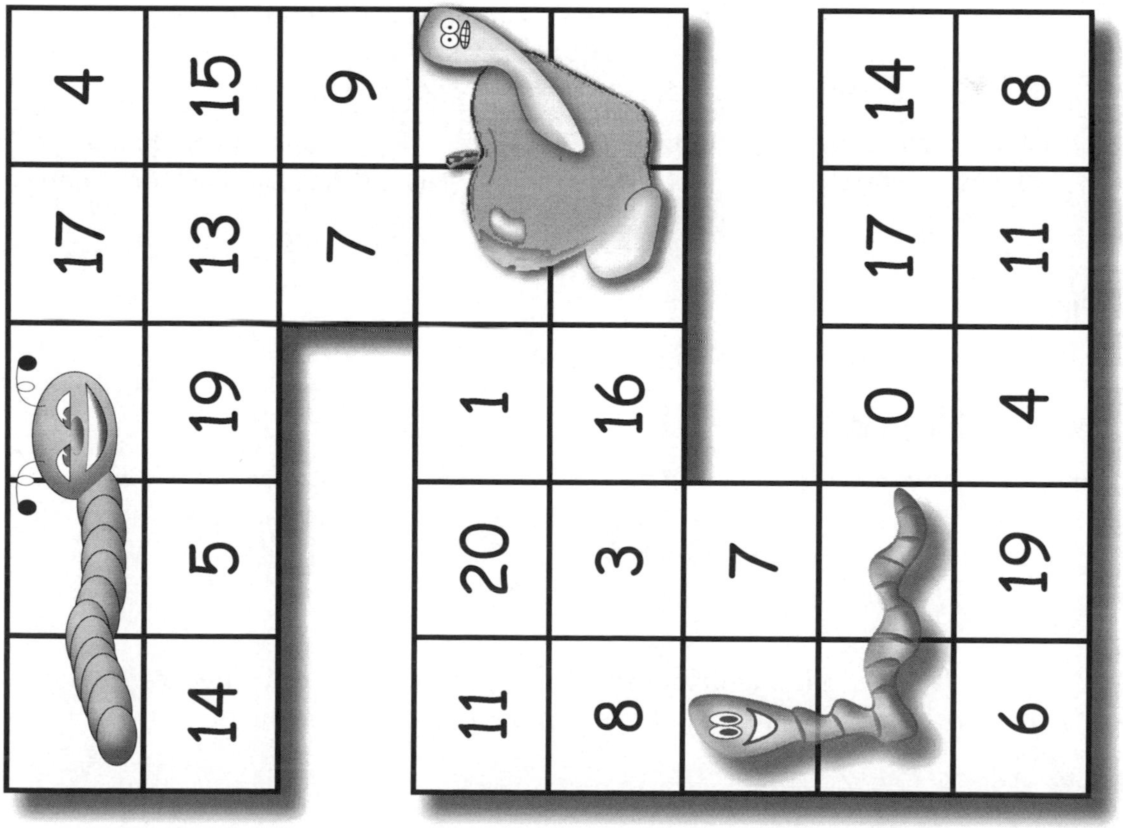
17 4
14 5 19 13 15
7 9
11 20 1
8 3 16
7
0 17 14
6 19 4 11 8

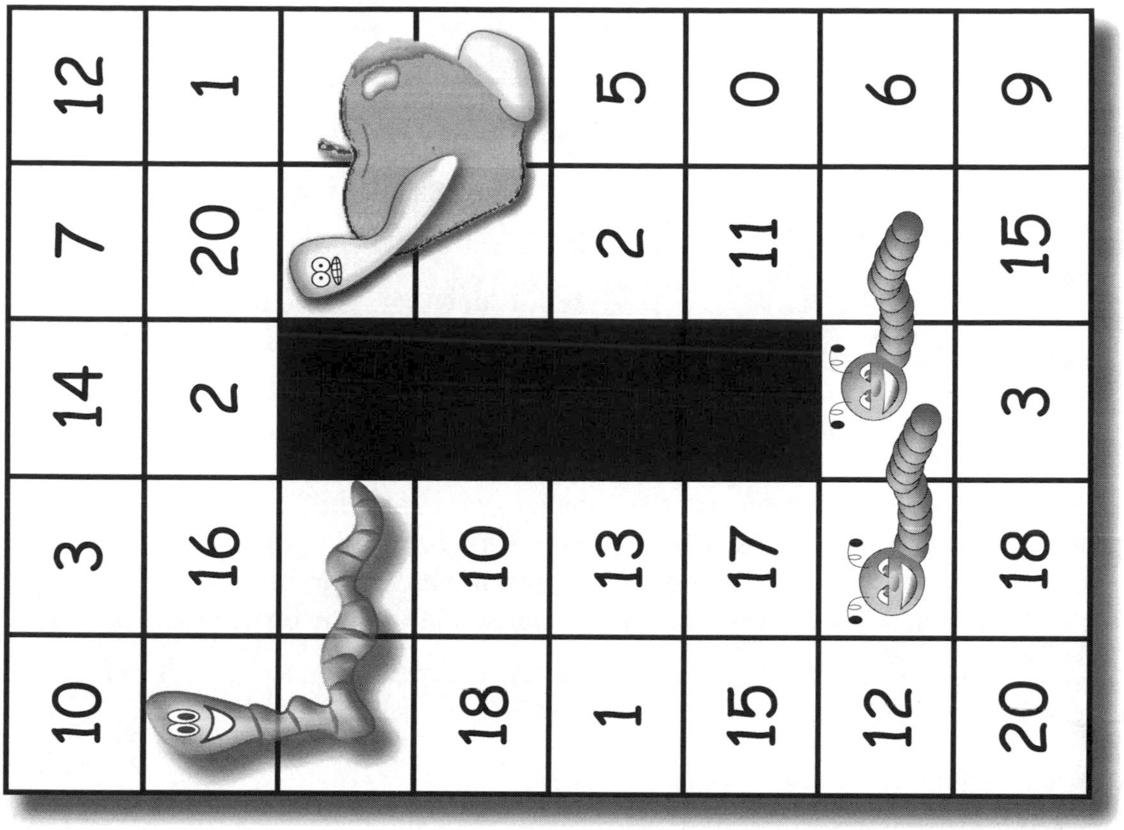
10 3 14 7 12
16 2 20 1
18 10
1 13 2 5
15 17 11 0
12 6
20 18 3 15 9

Robot Wars

Focus

Robot Wars is a game for two or more players which practices recall of addition and subtraction facts to twenty.

What you need

▶ Playing cards (picture cards removed)

▶ Counters (a different colour for each player)

▶ Robot Wars game board

How to play

When the picture cards have been removed, the remaining cards are shuffled and placed face-down, within reach of all the players. Player 1 turns over two cards and can either find the total or the difference between the two numbers. Player 1 then writes this number in any of the blank squares on the game board.

Player 2 then turns over two cards and works out the total and the difference. They can then write either number in any of the remaining blank squares on the board.

Players continue to take cards in turn and write their numbers on the board. However, if a player can write their number next to an identical number already on the board (such as a seven next to a seven or a three next to a three) they can then cover both those numbers with counters. Numbers that are not identical cannot be written in an adjacent square unless it is the only option left on the board. If a player is able to place counters they get another turn.

When all the cards have been used, shuffle them and place them back down in a pile within reach of all the players. Play continues until all the squares on the board have been used.

How to win

The player with the most counters on the robot is the winner.

Rule changes / Next steps

▶ As a challenge, players could be asked to multiply each number by ten before adding or subtracting the two numbers. So if a player turns a three and an eight they could calculate:
30 + 80 = 110   or   80 − 30 = 50   instead of   3 + 8 = 11   or   8 − 3 = 5.

▶ Use these facts to demonstrate that addition of two numbers can be done in any order and subtraction of one number from another cannot.

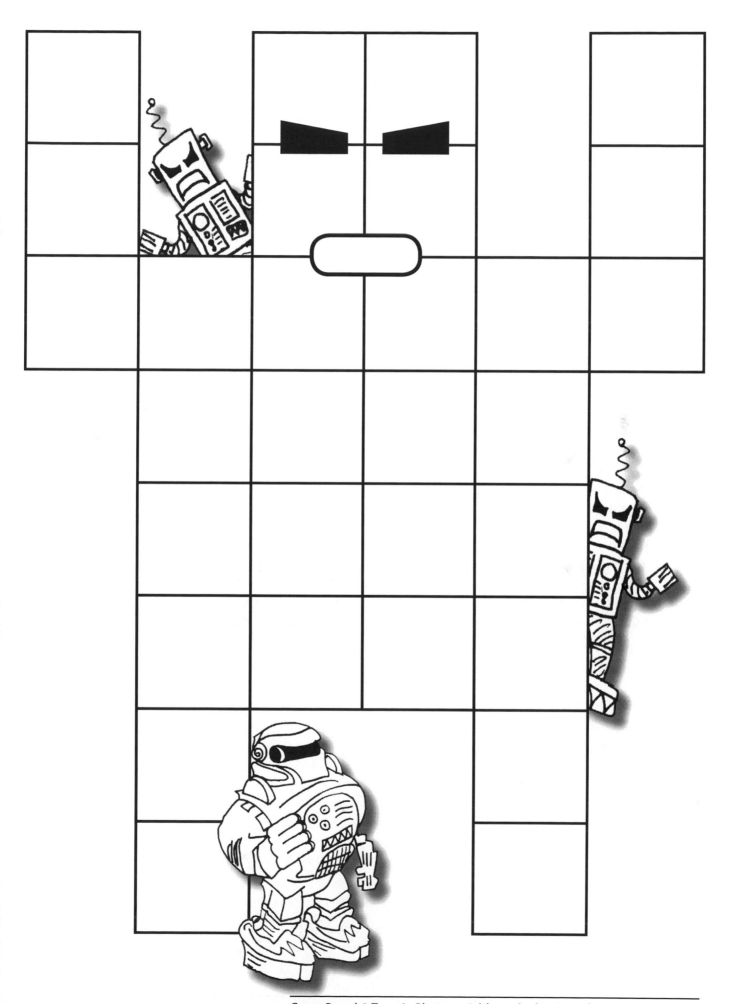

Game Board © Tarquin Photocopiable under licence – for terms see page 2

Odds

Focus

Odds is a game for two or more players which practices adding and subtracting two-digit numbers and ones up to fifty whilst recognising odd and even numbers.

What you need

▶ Playing cards (tens and picture cards removed)

▶ Counter

▶ Odds game board

How to play

When the tens and picture cards have been removed from the pack the remaining cards are shuffled and dealt out equally between the players. Each player then places their cards in a pile face-down in front of them. Player 1 starts the game by turning over a card, placing it face-up next to their pile and then moving the counter to the matching number on the game board. If the number is odd Player 1 can turn over another card and place it on top whilst saying the total of the two cards. The counter is moved to the matching number on the game board and if the answer is odd again, Player 1 keeps going. As soon as an even total is made Player 1 must stop and Player 2 turns over a card.

For example

Player 1 turns over the three of hearts so they move the counter to the matching number on the game board. This is an odd number so Player 1 turns over another card. This time the eight of spades is turned over and placed on top of the three. Player 1 says the total eleven as 3 + 8 = 11 and moves the counter. This is also an odd number so Player 1 gets to turn over another card. The nine of hearts is turned over by Player 1 and placed on top of the eight. Player 1 says the running total of twenty as 11 + 9 = 20 and again moves the counter to the matching number on the game board. This time an even number has been made so it is Player 2's turn to turn over a card.

Play continues in this way with odd totals getting that player another turn but an even total allowing the next player to take a turn. When the total goes past thirty, the counter is moved back to the start and the next card starts the running total again from zero. If an incorrect total is given, players could miss that turn and have to place the card at the bottom of their pile. Remember, it is the odd or even total that is important, not whether the number on the card itself is odd or even.

How to win

The first player to finish all their cards is the winner.

Rule changes / Next steps

▶ Play Odds 50 in exactly the same way but for an extra challenge play can also include the tens and picture cards.

▶ Start at the higher number and subtract, following the same rules.

▶ If a player lands exactly on the finishing number with the turn of a card they win the game. Alternatively, this player must pick up all their cards and start with a full pile again.

Instruction Sheet © Tarquin Photocopiable under licence – for terms see page 2

Odds 30

1	2	3	4	5	6	7	8	9	10
11	12	13	14	15	16	17	18	19	20
21	22	23	24	25	26	27	28	29	30

Game Board © Tarquin Photocopiable under licence – for terms see page 2

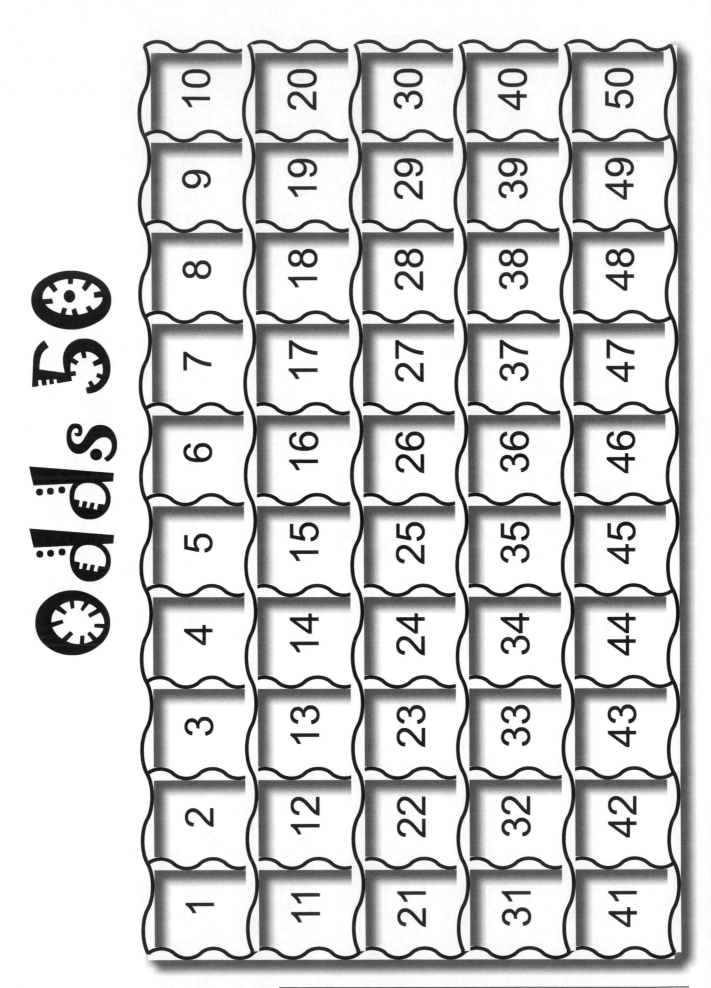

Odds 50

1	2	3	4	5	6	7	8	9	10
11	12	13	14	15	16	17	18	19	20
21	22	23	24	25	26	27	28	29	30
31	32	33	34	35	36	37	38	39	40
41	42	43	44	45	46	47	48	49	50

Game Board © Tarquin Photocopiable under licence – for terms see page 2

The Hundred Dash

Focus

The Hundred Dash is a game for two or more players which practices adding and subtracting two-digit numbers and ones with numbers up to one hundred.

What you need

▶ Playing cards

▶ Counters (a different colour for each player)

▶ The Hundred Dash game board

How to play

Firstly the cards are shuffled and then placed in a pile, face-down and within reach of all the players. Each player starts with a counter of their own colour at the start of the game board (first diagram).

Player 1 starts the game by turning over a card and placing it face-up in front of them.

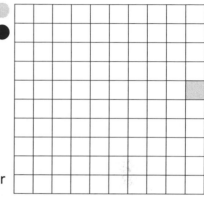

For example

As seen in the second diagram, Player 1 (black counter) has turned over a three, followed by Player 2 (grey counter), who has turned over an eight.

Play continues in this fashion, with players taking it in turns to pick up a card and add that amount to the number underneath their counter. So if Player 1 turned over a nine on their next turn they would have to do 3 + 9 = 12 and move to that position on the game board.

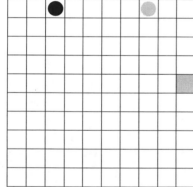

Players must do all their mental calculations before moving their counter. The player must also give the correct answer to move their counter, otherwise it remains in the same place on the game board.

If a player lands on top of another player's counter below fifty they send their opponent back to the start. If the counter is beyond fifty then it is sent back to that halfway square.

How to win

The first player to land on or go past a hundred (finish line) is the winner.

Rule changes / Next steps

▶ Start at a hundred, subtracting the value of the card, with the finish line at zero.

▶ Include the tens and picture cards for some two digit addition and subtraction calculations.

▶ Players have a boost counter that they can play once in the game to double the number on their card. This could be played before or after the card is turned over.

▶ If a player turns over an odd card they add the value of the card but if they turn over an even card they add ten regardless of its value.

The Hundred Dash

1	2	3	4	5	6	7	8	9	10
11	12	13	14	15	16	17	18	19	20
21	22	23	24	25	26	27	28	29	30
31	32	33	34	35	36	37	38	39	40
41	42	43	44	45	46	47	48	49	50
51	52	53	54	55	56	57	58	59	60
61	62	63	64	65	66	67	68	69	70
71	72	73	74	75	76	77	78	79	80
81	82	83	84	85	86	87	88	89	90
91	92	93	94	95	96	97	98	99	100

Game Board © Tarquin Photocopiable under licence – for terms see page 2

Hooked!

Focus

Hooked! is a game for two players which practices adding and subtracting one and two-digit numbers up to forty and sixty.

What you need

▶ Playing cards

▶ Counter

▶ Hooked! game board

How to play

The cards are shuffled and placed in a pile, face-down between both players. Decide who is counting forwards and who is counting backwards. The player counting forwards moves from left to right along the game board and the player counting backwards moves from right to left. Place a counter on the middle number of the game board.

Players take it in turns to turn over a card and that number is added to or subtracted from (depending on the player's direction of play) the number underneath the counter.

For example

Player 1 (adding) turns over a six. They say 20 + 6 = 26, and then move to that square on the game board. Player 2 (subtracting) turns over a queen. They say 26 − 12 = 14 and move the counter to that square.

Players must perform the mental calculation before moving the counter, and a correct answer must be given in order to move. When all the cards have been used, shuffle them and place them back down in a pile so that play can continue.

How to win

Player 2 (subtracting) hooks the fish and wins by getting the counter to land on or go past zero whilst Player 1 (adding) hooks the fish and wins by getting the counter to land on or go past forty (or sixty if playing Hooked! 60).

Rule changes / Next steps

▶ Change roles and play again so both players practice their addition and subtraction skills.

▶ Play for a set number of turns and the player who is closest to their end of the game board wins.

▶ For Hooked! 60 players turn over a card and must double its value before adding or subtracting this amount to the number underneath the counter.

▶ Allow players to do the calculation by counting up or down whilst moving the counter at the same time.

▶ Encourage children to investigate patterns in adding and subtracting numbers, such as:
5 + 6 = 11   15 + 6 = 21   25 + 6 = 31   so   35 + 6 = __   and so on.

Instruction Sheet © Tarquin Photocopiable under licence – for terms see page 2

Hooked!

40

0

20

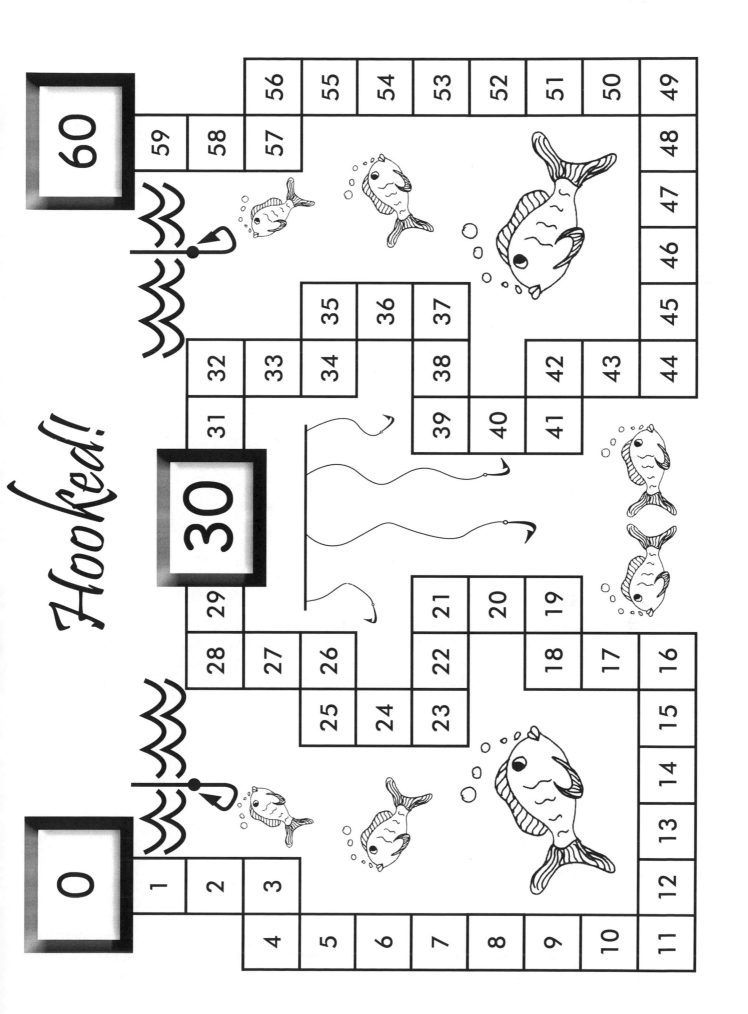

Hooked!

Dare!

Focus

Dare is a game for two or more players which practices adding and subtracting one and two-digit numbers up to fifty.

What you need

▶ Playing cards

▶ Counters (a different colour for each player)

▶ Dare! game board

How to play

Firstly, the cards are shuffled and placed in a pile, face-down and within reach of all the players. The players' counters are placed on the number fifty on the game board, which is the starting position. Player 1 takes a card and then subtracts this number from the number underneath their counter (which, in this first instance, is fifty), moving their counter to that number on the game board. Player 1 must then decide whether to play safe, stop and pass the cards to the next player or to 'dare' and turn over another card. If Player 1 decides to dare and turn over another card then:

▶ if the card is the same colour they can continue by subtracting the value of the card from the number underneath their counter;

▶ if the card is a different colour they must go back to the first grey **DARE SQUARE** they reach by moving backwards along the game board.

If Player 1 decides to stop then play goes to Player 2. Play continues with players taking a card, subtracting its value from the number underneath their counter, and moving their counter to the new total.

Players must do all their mental calculations before moving the counter. If a player gives an incorrect answer then they are unable to move their counter on that turn. If a player lands on top of another counter, the counter landed on is moved back to the start or to the first grey DARE SQUARE reached by moving back along the board - whichever is agreed by the players before the game begins.

How to win

The first player to land on or go past zero (the finish line) is the winner.

Rule changes / Next steps

▶ Play Dare 30 by taking the higher number cards (seven and above) out of the pack to make players subtract more of the smaller numbers.

▶ Play as an addition game, starting at zero and adding up to the finish line.

▶ Each player starts with a dare counter and is allowed to use it once at any time during the game. The dare counter forces another player to dare and carry on even when they have decided to stop. The dared player must then carry on for two more cards. The same rules apply as outlined previously. However, if they turn over a card of a different colour they must go back to the first grey dare square they reach by moving backwards along the game board from where they started that turn.

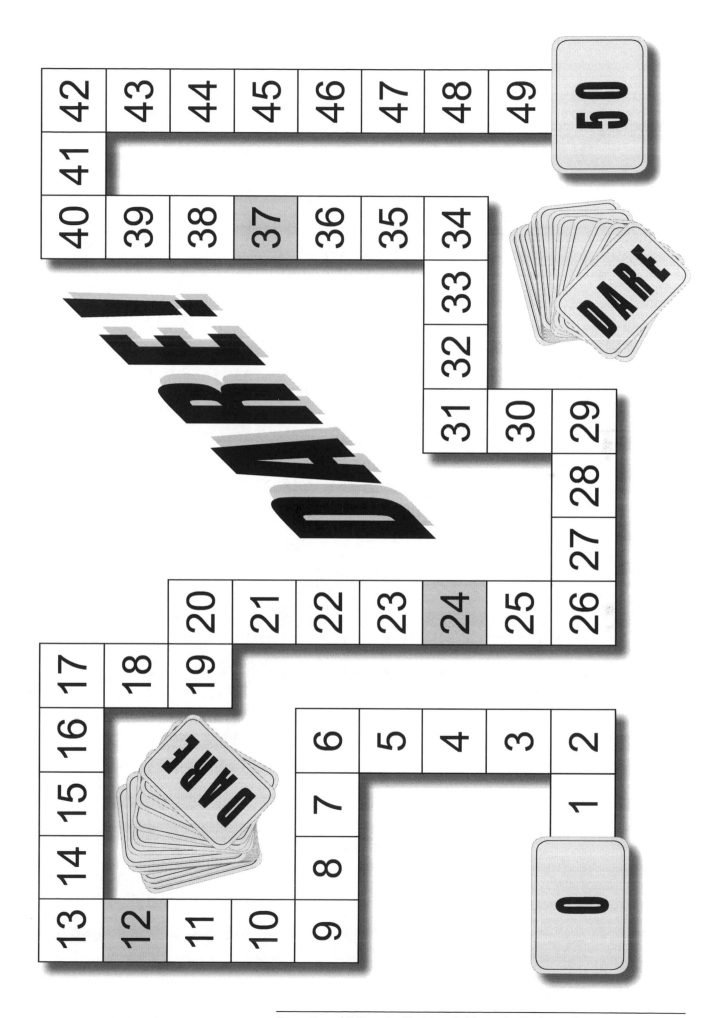

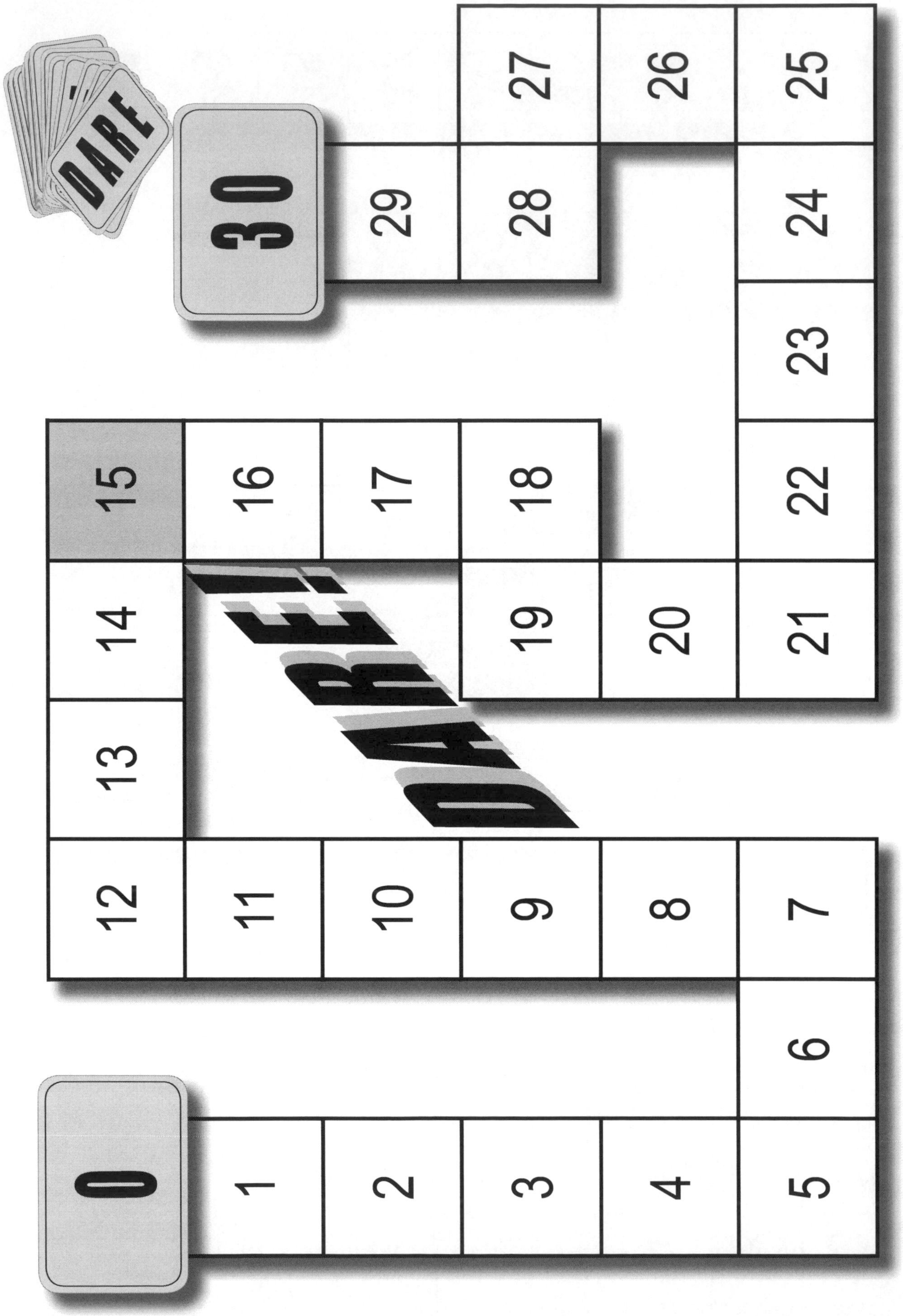

DARE

30

27

26

25

29

28

24

23

15

16

17

18

22

14

19

20

21

DARE! DARE

13

12

11

10

9

8

7

6

0

1

2

3

4

5

Speed Seekers

Focus

Speed Seekers is a game for two or more players which practices adding and subtracting two-digit numbers up to one hundred.

What you need

▶ Playing cards (aces to fours removed)

▶ Counters (a different colour for each player)

▶ Speed Seekers game board

▶ How to play

When the smaller cards have been removed from the pack the remainder are shuffled and placed in a pile, face-down and within reach of all the players. Player 1 takes a card from the top of the pack and doubles its value to get a total. They then subtract this total from the number under their counter (on the first turn, this is the starting value of one hundred). On performing the calculation correctly, they then move their counter to the relevant square on the game board.

For example

Player 1 (grey counter) turns over a six. First, they calculate double six, or 2 x 6 = 12. They then calculate 100 – 12 = 88 and move their counter to that position on the game board.

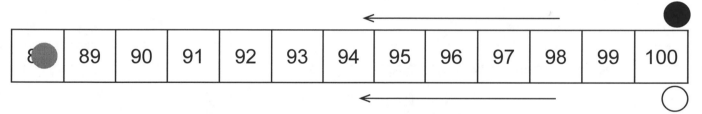

| 8 | 89 | 90 | 91 | 92 | 93 | 94 | 95 | 96 | 97 | 98 | 99 | 100 |

Play goes to Player 2 who turns over a nine. Calculating double nine, or 2 x 9 = 18, and then 100 – 18 = 82, they move their counter to number eighty-two on the board. Play continues in this way, with players taking a card, doubling its value, and subtracting this total from the number underneath their counter.

Players must do all their mental calculations before moving their counter. They must also give the correct answer to move their counter otherwise it remains where it is on the game board.

If a player lands on a Speed Seeker (grey) square they can choose to either move forward nine spaces or move any one other player backwards nine squares. If a player lands on top of another counter, the counter landed on is moved back to the first Speed Seeker square they reach by moving backwards along the game board.

How to win

The first player to land on or go past zero (the finish line) on the game board is the winner.

Rule changes / Next steps

▶ For Speed Seekers 50 the value of the card is subtracted from the number beneath the counter. Cards ten and above can be removed to make the subtractions easier.

▶ Play as an addition game, starting at the lower number and adding up to the finish line.

Instruction Sheet © Tarquin Photocopiable under licence – for terms see page 2

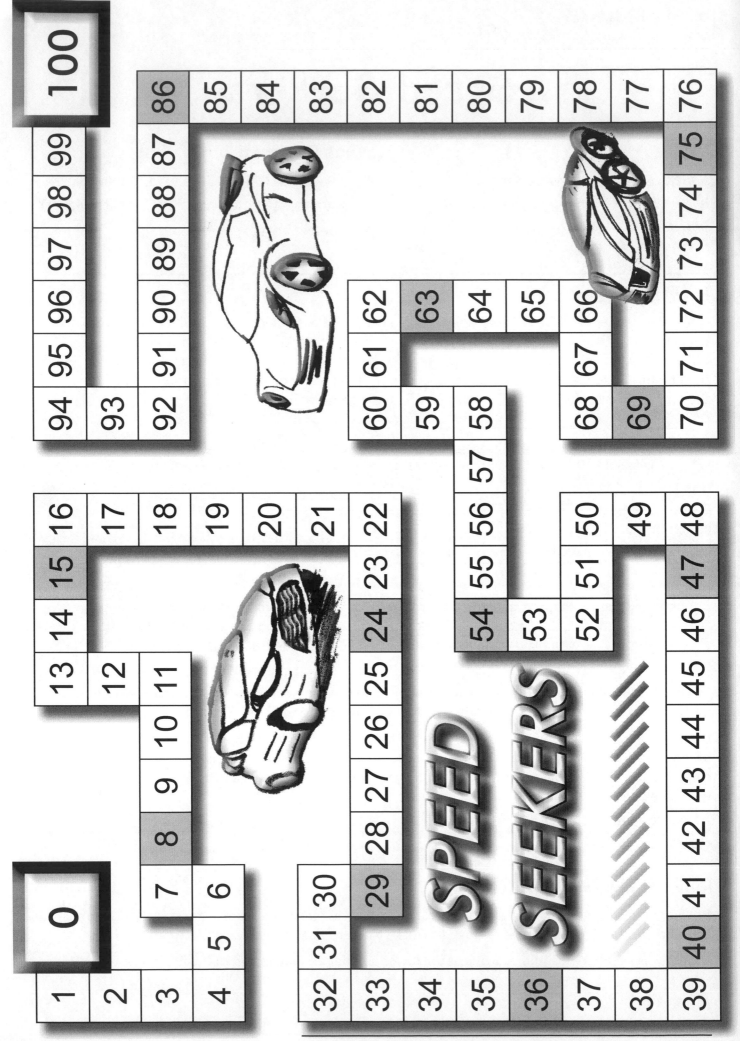

SPEED SEEKERS

Game Board © Tarquin Photocopiable under licence – for terms see page 2

SPEED SEEKERS

| 42 | 43 | 44 | 45 | 46 | 47 | 48 | 49 | 50 |

| 41 |

40	39	38	37	36	35	34
						33
						32
					31	30	29
							28
							27
20	21	22	23	24	25	26

17	18	19
16		
15		6	5	4	3	2
14		7				1
13	12	11	10	9		0

Trios

Focus

Trios is a game for four to six players which can be used to practice becoming more efficient in a range of mental methods with numbers up to fifty.

What you need

▶ Playing cards

▶ Counters (a different colour for each player)

▶ Trios game board

How to play

Player 1 turns over any number of cards and could be asked to add, subtract or multiply them to get an answer, depending on what skill or knowledge from the Year 2 programme of study the game is being used to practice. If the player gets the answer correct they can place a counter of their own colour in a circle on the game board.

Player 2 then turns over one or more cards and performs a similar calculation. Play continues in this way with players taking it in turns to take one or more cards, answer questions and place counters on the game board. If a player gives an incorrect answer, they are unable to place a counter on that turn.

How to win

The first player to make a Trio is the winner. Trios can either be in a triangle or in a straight line as shown in the diagram.

Remove all the counters and play again.

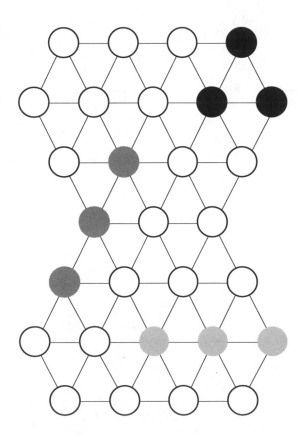

Rule changes / Next steps

▶ Players continue to try and make Trios until all the spaces are covered or until the players agree that no more can be made. Players score three points for every Trio they make and the winner is the player with the most points at the end of the game.

▶ Restrict players to making only triangles or straight lines to win the game rather than allowing both.

TRIOS

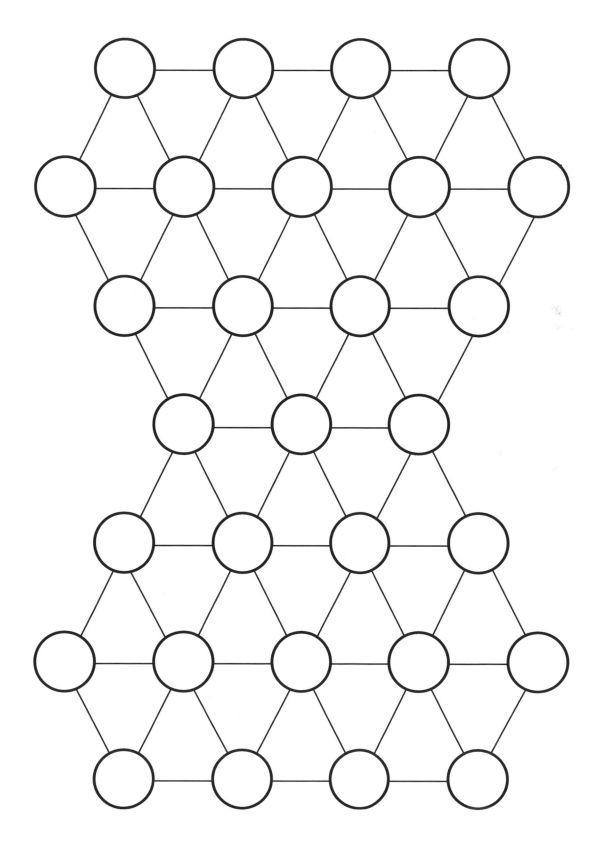

Monster Mash-Up

Focus

Monster Mash-up is a game for two to six players which can be used to practice becoming more efficient in a range of mental methods with numbers up to one hundred.

What you need

▶ Playing cards (cards 1 – 5)

▶ Counters (one for each player)

▶ Monster Mash-Up game board

▶ Question cards, if using (see Next Steps, below)

How to play

When the cards from six upwards have been removed from the pack the remaining cards are shuffled and placed in a pile, face-down and within reach of all the players. Players then choose a monster and place their counter on it, ready for the start of the game.

Player 1 is asked a question by the question master to practice recall of facts or any skill within the Year 2 programme of study. If answered correctly Player 1 turns over a card and can then move the same number of spaces on the game board. If the answer is incorrect the player is not allowed to move their counter. The other players are then asked questions in turn. If correct they can turn over a card and move the same number of spaces on the game board.

Black holes

Players must try and avoid the black holes in various positions, since landing on one sends them back to their monster at the start of the game.

How to win

The first player to land on or go beyond an end square is the winner.

Rule changes / Next steps

▶ Players can move one bonus square if they can answer a question that another player has answered incorrectly.

▶ Different kinds of question may be selected, dependent, for example, on what a particular child needs to practice, or on particular skills needed for assessment purposes.

▶ Players must turn the exact number to land on an end square and win the game.

▶ Use the set of mixed mental questions provided. Put them face-down on the table for children to pick at random, read aloud and then answer. Alternatively, pass them to an appointed question master to read out.

Instruction Sheet © Tarquin Photocopiable under licence – for terms see page 2

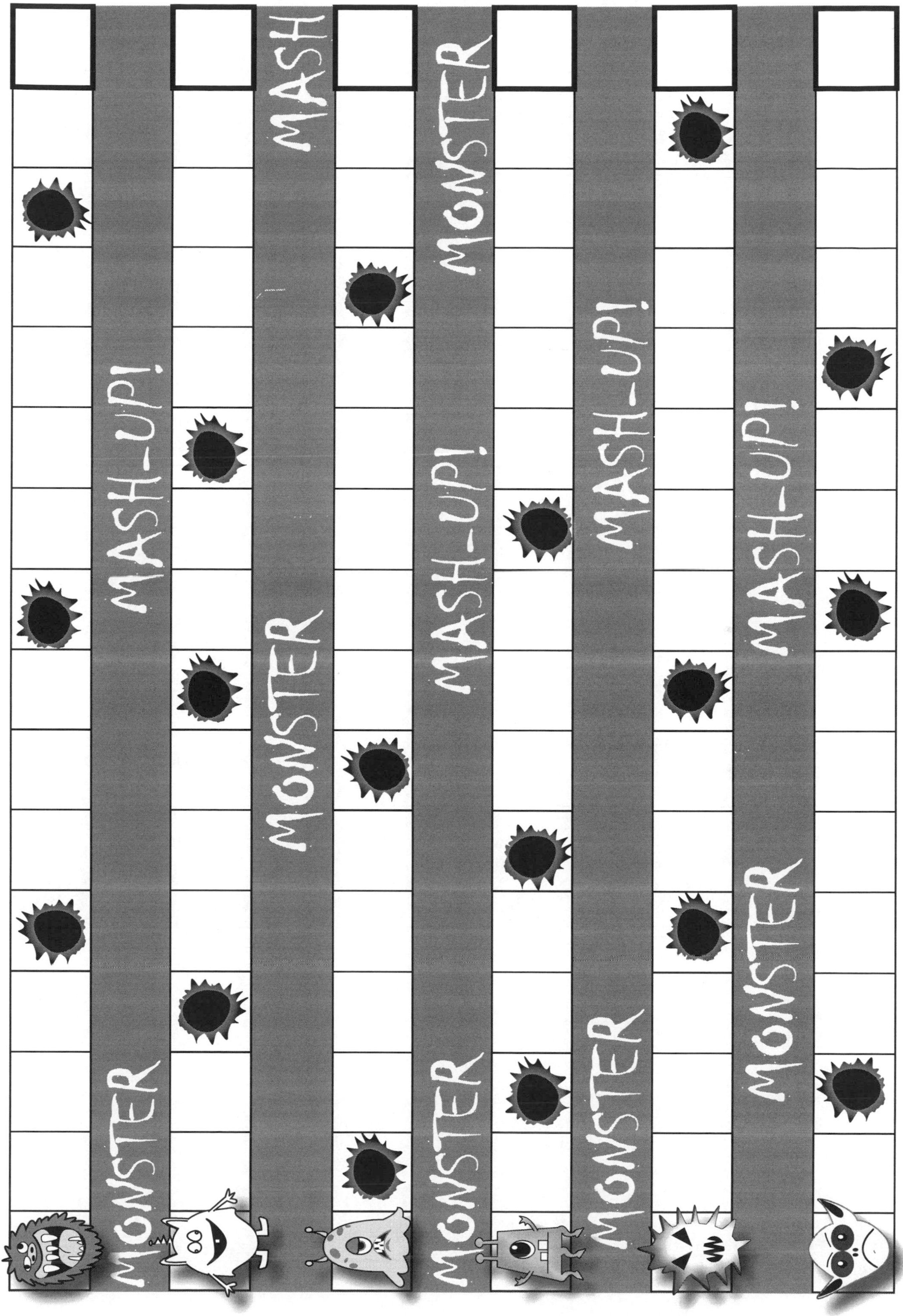
MONSTER
MASH-UP!
MONSTER
MASH
MONSTER
MASH-UP!
MONSTER
MONSTER
MASH-UP!
MONSTER
MASH-UP!

What two numbers come next? 12, 14, 16, 18, …, …	What two numbers come next? 39, 37, 35, 33, …, …	What is 10 more than 74?	What is 10 less than 37?
What is 1 more than 29?	What is 1 less than 40?	What is the 3 worth in 38?	What is the value of the underlined digit in 24?
True or False 66 is more than 45	True or False 80 is less than 92	Write the number fifty-seven in figures	Write the number seventy in figures
85 = 50 + __	46 = 30 + __	Take ten away from 63	Take six away from 30
What is 7 more than 28?	What is 9 less than 50?	Add 6 to 57	Subtract 8 from 42
54 + 40 =	93 – 80 =	76 + 7 =	64 – 6
43 + 15	99 - 22	15 = __ + 8	7 = 12 – __
__ + 30 = 41	__ – 10 = 4	What is the sum of 28 and 11?	What is the difference between 18 and 23?

2 + 7 + 3 =	5 + 6 + 5 =	10 = 2 + __ + 3	__ + 8 + 3 = 20
3 x 5 =	10 x 8 =	2 x 4 =	10 x 5 =
8 x 2 =	5 x 7 =	40 ÷ 10 =	14 ÷ 2 =
How many lots of 5 are there in 30?	How many groups of 10 can you make from 100?	If 6 x 2 = 12, what is 12 x 2?	If 6 x 10 = 60, what is 12 x 10?
6 = __ x 2	__ ÷ 5 = 3	7 = 70 ÷ __	2 x __ = 10
What is ½ of 12?	What is ½ of 20?	What is ½ of 4?	What is ½ of 100?
True or False ½ is bigger than ¼	True or False Two quarters is smaller than a half	What is ¼ of 12?	What is ¼ of 8?
How many halves are there in a whole one?	What two numbers come next? 1, 1½, 2, 2½, …, …	Half a number is 3. What is the number?	Half a number is 5. What is the number?

Tarquin Mathematics Resources

Tarquin has more than a thousand product lines to support and enrich mathematics. You can browse them at **www.tarquingroup.com**.

To make it easy to buy what you need to really use this book, we have some special packages online — put the keyword ACE into the quick search box to see the full range at once.

▶ Packs of Playing Cards - Special ACE prices

▶ Coloured Counters

▶ Beads

Other Tarquin Products designed for you

Books

First Tables Colouring Book

Second Tables Colouring Book

Arithmetic Arithmetic

Mathematical Vocabulary 1

    and many, many more ...

Posters

One Million Poster

Multiples Poster

Equal Parts Poster

    and many, many more ...

Dice and other Manipulatives

Excellent prices on 12-sided and 10-sided dice classroom packs — ideal for mental mathematics

Practical Arithmetic and Operations Dice Packs

Pentominoes, tangrams, Cuisenaire Rods, Polygons and much much more.

Tarquin, Suite 74, 17 Holywell Hill, St Albans, AL1 1DT
Tel: +44 (0)1727833866 Fax: +44 (0)845 456 6385
www.tarquingroup.com   Follow us on Twitter @TarquinGroup